Biomes
of North
America

A Journey into a Lake

by Rebecca L. Johnson

with illustrations by Phyllis V. Saroff

 CAROLRHODA BOOKS, INC./MINNEAPOLIS

Carolrhoda Books, Inc.
A division of Lerner Publishing Group
241 First Avenue North
Minneapolis, Minnesota 55401 U.S.A.

Website address: www.lernerbooks.com

Library of Congress Cataloging-in-Publication Data

Johnson, Rebecca L.
   A journey into a lake / by Rebecca L. Johnson; illustrations by
Phyllis V. Saroff.
     p.   cm. — (Biomes of North America)
   Includes index.
   Summary: Takes readers on a journey into a lake, showing
examples of how the animals and plants are connected and
dependent on each other and on the lake's freshwater
environment.
   ISBN: 1-57505-594-5 (lib. bdg. : alk. paper)
   1. Lake ecology—Juvenile literature. 2. Lakes—Juvenile literature.
[1. Lake ecology. 2. Lakes. 3. Ecology.] I. Saroff, Phyllis V., ill.
II. Title. III. Series.
QH541.5.L3J62 2004
577.63—dc22   2003015726

Manufactured in the United States of America
1 2 3 4 5 6 — JR — 09 08 07 06 05 04

Words
to Know

BACTERIA (*bak-TEE-ree-uh*)—microscopic, one-celled living things found almost everywhere

BARBELS (*BAHR-behls*)—whiskerlike feelers on the faces of bullheads and other catfish

DAM—a wall or other barrier that is built across a body of water, such as a river

DECOMPOSER (*dee-cuhm-POH-zur*)—a living thing that breaks down dead plants, animals, and other natural wastes and returns their valuable nutrients to the environment

FOOD CHAIN—the connection among living things that shows what eats what in an ecosystem

MIGRATE (*MYE-grate*)—to move from one place to another during certain seasons of the year. Most animals migrate to find better weather and more food.

NYMPH (*nihmf*)—an insect that is not yet an adult

PREDATOR (*PREH-duh-tur*)—an animal that hunts and eats other animals

PREY (*pray*)—an animal that is hunted and eaten by other animals

SCAVENGER (*SKA-vuhn-jur*)—an animal that does not hunt but eats whatever it can find, including dead animals and other waste

TADPOLE—a frog that is not yet an adult. Tadpoles have fins and gills, like fish.

TALONS—large, sharp claws

TERRITORY (*TAIR-ih-tohr-ee*)—the area in which an animal lives and feeds. Some animals are very protective of their territories.

WATER BIOME (*WAHT-ur BYE-ohm*)—a major community of living things in a water-based area, such as a lake or a river

Wisps of mist

rising at dawn

In the morning light, mist hangs over the water like steam. A beaver sits on the bank, eating the bark of a tree branch. Dead leaves rustle close by. The beaver stops chewing and sniffs the air. Sensing danger, he scrambles into the water. With a slap of his tail, the beaver dives deep into the safety of the lake.

5

A lake's still surface reflects the mountains around it.

The lake is a cool stretch of water rimmed with green. On a breezy day, wind stirs the water, sending ripples across its surface. But on a calm day, the water is so still that it reflects the sky and the landscape like a huge mirror.

Lakes are pools of freshwater that fill low spots in the land. Some lakes are shallow and small enough to swim across. Others are big and broad and hundreds of feet deep.

You can find lakes almost anywhere. Some dot rolling prairies. Others are tucked away among high mountain peaks or hidden in dense forests.

Some lakes are broad stretches ringed with plants.

Chances are you've seen a lake—or a pond, which really is just a very small, very shallow lake. Maybe you've seen a river or a wetland too. If you have visited the coast, you may have walked along the edge of an estuary, where a river meets the ocean. Or you might have strolled along the ocean's shore.

Water biomes range from the crashing ocean (above) to rippling rivers (left) to marshy wetlands (below).

Lakes, rivers, wetlands, estuaries, and the ocean make up the earth's water biomes. A water biome is a water-based region that is home to a unique group of living things. These living things are all adapted, or specially suited, to living in that region.

Each biome's living things, from tiny microscopic creatures to large plants and animals, form a community. Each member of that community depends on the others. All of these living things, in turn, depend on the water—fresh or salty, moving or still—that forms their watery home. They swim through it, find food in it, and are sometimes carried from place to place by it. Without the water, they could not survive.

Every creature in a water biome depends on the community's other members. Frogs eat insects such as dragonflies. Dragonflies, in turn, eat smaller insects.

Lakes form in different ways. A mountain lake forms where water from melted snow fills a valley. Some lakes lie over natural springs, where water bubbles up from underground.

A series of lakes fills the dips in a green valley (right), while another lake nestles in a desert canyon (below).

Many lakes form along rivers. This can happen where a river flows into a large, deep place in the land. It can also happen when a river is blocked by a dam. The water backs up behind the dam, creating a lake.

This large lake formed behind a dam in a river.

Some dams are built by people. But beavers are also dam builders. The beaver that was eating a branch on the bank created the lake where he lives. Years ago, he built a dam of tree branches and mud across a river. The lake that formed behind the dam became the beaver's home. It is also home to many other living things.

Beavers work hard to build the piles of sticks and mud that make up their dams (top and right). These dams create the lakes where beavers and their families live.

12

Beavers use their huge, chisel-shaped front teeth to cut down the trees and branches that they use to build dams.

Out in the lake, the beaver is paddling toward shore. He's coming back to finish breakfast. Let's follow the beaver on a journey into this clear, sparkling lake.

The beaver rests near the lakeshore before getting back to work.

Birches grow along the lakeshore, close to the water's edge.

All around the lake, the air feels fresh and cool. The morning mist has lifted. Golden sunbeams dance on the water's surface. The sun has climbed above tops of the trees around the lake.

Many of the trees are birches. They thrive in the lakeshore's damp soil. Their bright green leaves flutter and dance in the breeze.

The leaves of trees that grow around the lake come in many different shapes and sizes.

alder   willow   cottonwood

Growing among the birches are cottonwood, willow, and alder trees. Their leaves gleam in the morning sun.

The leaves of trees and other green plants use sunlight to make their own food. The plants, in turn, are food for many kinds of animals in and around the lake. Plants are an essential first link in the lake's food chain.

Tall trees surround the lake like a green ribbon.

Pointing its beak skyward, a bittern hides by blending into the grasses around its lake home.

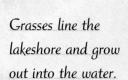

Grasses line the lakeshore and grow out into the water.

Tall grasses also grow along the lakeshore. Sedges, rushes, reeds, and cattails form a fringe of bright green that stretches right down to the water's edge. With every puff of wind, thousands of long, slender leaves rub and rustle together. It sounds like the grasses are whispering to each other all around the lake.

And look—see how many of the leaves have been chewed? Caterpillars, beetles, and other bugs creep and crawl among the grasses, eating as they go.

The beaver reaches the shore and clambers out of the water. A red-winged blackbird swoops down and lands on a cattail above the beaver's head. *Check—check—kong-kar-eeee!* The bird shrieks out its harsh call. It's trying to scare the beaver away. The bird's nest is nearby, well hidden among the whispering grasses.

The nest holds a treasure of pale green, darkly spotted eggs. The mother bird sits on the nest to keep the eggs warm. When the eggs hatch, the blackbird chicks will dine on insects that their parents catch for them.

A red-winged blackbird perches on a cattail near its nest.

Lake water teems with plankton. a collection of microscopic life-forms.

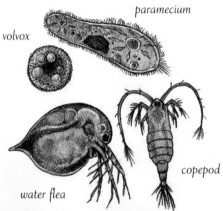

volvox

paramecium

water flea

copepod

Look into the water. The beaver stirred up the mud when he came ashore. As the mud settles, you can see that the shallow edge of the lake is crowded with plants too.

Delicate leaves sprout from the slender stems of crowfoot, hornwort, and mare's tail. Strong roots anchor these water plants to the lake bottom.

Plump snails with spiral-shaped shells creep slowly through this underwater forest. Tadpoles and crayfish also hide among the stems.

A hungry crayfish prowls the shallows for food.

18

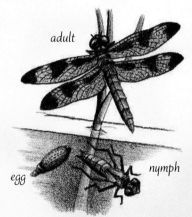

They are hiding for a reason. Ferocious predators hunt in the shallows. Dragonfly nymphs and giant diving beetles lie in wait to make a meal out of tadpoles, minnows, and other small creatures that pass by. With lightning speed, they grab their prey in pincerlike jaws.

Overhead on the water's surface, silvery water striders zoom back and forth like skaters on ice. They devour flies and other insects that are unlucky enough to land near them on the water.

A diving beetle snags an unlucky salamander *(top left)*. Water striders move across the lake's surface with ease *(top right)*, while a dragonfly nymph rests on the rocky bottom *(bottom right)*.

From farther out on the lake comes a low, hollow-sounding *GUNK!* Moments later, the sound comes again. Two large green frogs are out there, croaking loudly. Each is warning the other to stay out of its territory.

The frogs are sitting on the leaves of water lilies. These big, saucerlike leaves float on the water's surface.

Tiny minnows, swimming in groups called schools, hide in the shadows of water lily leaves.

The water lilies are blooming. Their flowers are full of sweet liquid. Bees and other insects fly in for a drink. But if they are not careful, the sharp-eyed frogs will catch them on their long, sticky tongues.

The flowers of water lilies attract bees and other insects with bright colors and sweet scents.

21

Beyond the water lilies, a pair of mallard ducks flies in and lands on the lake. The mallards use their broad bills to skim duckweed from the water's surface. The pinhead-sized leaves of duckweed are full of tiny air pockets that keep them afloat. The floating duckweed catches plenty of sunlight—but it also makes it an easy meal for hungry ducks.

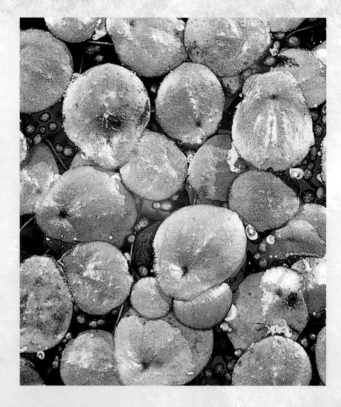

Tiny duckweed plants float on the lake's surface (top), *where they are scooped up by a mallard duck and her chicks* (right).

The webbing between a duck's toes helps it paddle more powerfully through the water.

Several pintails and a wigeon arrive to join the mallards. As they paddle around, the birds upend themselves—with heads underwater and tails in the air—to reach crowfoot and other plants on the lake bottom.

The lake is home to hundreds of ducks and geese. Some live here year-round. Others, such as the pintails and wigeons, are summer visitors. In the spring, they migrate up from lakes farther south to build nests near the water and raise their families of chicks. In the fall, they fly south again to spend the winter in warmer climates.

Hungry ducks upend, with tails pointing skyward and necks stretching down to reach food below.

23

The beaver stands beside a freshly cut tree trunk. The tree will become food and building material.

Back on the shore, the beaver has finished eating the leaves and bark of the branch he started on this morning. He waddles back into the trees for another. He sinks his powerful teeth into the trunk of a small tree. In less than a minute, he has cut it down.

With a few more quick bites, the beaver gnaws off a big branch. But he doesn't eat this one. The beaver heads for the water with the branch in his mouth. He wades in and begins to swim, pulling the branch along. He's heading for the beaver lodge in the middle of the lake. The dome-shaped lodge, made of mud and sticks, is the beaver's home. He built it after his dam formed the lake.

The beaver tows his leafy treasure across the lake, setting a course for his lodge.

A merganser's long bill has jagged edges and a hooked tip—perfect for catching fish.

The beaver paddles past a pair of mergansers. These ducks are fish eaters, and they're looking for a meal.

Without warning, the mergansers dive. Ten seconds tick by, then twenty. Suddenly, the birds bob up on the surface. One has caught a small trout. The merganser tosses its head back and swallows the fish whole.

A diving merganser keeps its sharp eyes open for fish.

Many trout live in the lake. Fast and sleek, they zoom to the surface to snag insects that land on the water. They also eat dragonfly nymphs and crayfish. Large trout eat other fish—even other trout.

Brown trout swim swiftly through the lake's clear waters.

The shiny scales on a fish's body overlap like shingles on a roof.

Trout share their watery hunting grounds with other kinds of fish. Perch and bluegills cruise the shallows, snapping up underwater insects and minnows. If they aren't careful, though, they'll become food for bigger fish such as largemouth bass.

A school of bluegills cruises by (top), while a smallmouth bass lingers near a rocky ledge (right).

Pike lurk deeper, in thickets of underwater plants. Their long, slender bodies are shaped like arrows. Pike have big jaws and sharp teeth. Like tigers waiting in the trees, they dart out from hiding places to attack other fish, frogs—even baby ducks!

Pike hide in ambush among the fronds of underwater plants, waiting for unsuspecting prey to swim past.

Turtles sun themselves on the lakeshore or on partly sunken logs.

A painted turtle uses sturdy legs and webbed feet to swim.

The beaver nears his lodge in the middle of the lake. He tucks his head and dives. Both beaver and branch disappear beneath the surface.

Down, down, the beaver swims. Bubbles stream off his dense fur. A startled painted turtle makes a sharp turn to get out of the way.

As the beaver goes deeper, the water gets cooler and the light gradually fades. In the shadowy depths of the lake, the light is too dim for plants to grow. But there are other signs of life.

The beaver dives deeper with his branch. Flat tails and webbed back feet help beavers swim.

A bullhead lurks near the lake's dark bottom.

Roaming the lake bottom are bullheads. Using the long whiskerlike barbels on their faces, these fish feel their way around in the gloom. Bullheads are scavengers. They eat everything from crayfish and snails to dead fish.

Freshwater clams lie half buried in the soft lake-bottom mud. They draw water into their bodies, filter out tiny particles of food, and then pump the water back out.

Worms, bacteria, and other decomposers live in the muddy bottom too. They feed on the remains of dead plants and animals that slowly settle to the lake bottom. As the decomposers break down these wastes, they add nutrients to the water that other lake dwellers need to grow healthy and strong.

Freshwater clams help filter lake water by pumping it through their bodies.

The beaver lodge
stands in the
middle of the lake
like an island.

The beaver reaches the base of his lodge in the middle of the lake. Nearby is a mound of branches heaped on the lake bottom. The beaver swims over and jams the branch he's carrying into the pile.

During the winter, when the trees around the lake are bare and the grasses are dead, the beaver and his family will live off this supply of stored food.

The beaver swims into one of the lodge's tunnel-like entrances. The other end opens up into a little chamber in the middle of the lodge. The room is above the level of the lake. It is snug and dry.

Inside the room, the mother beaver is curled up with her three babies, called kits. At the moment, the kits are fast asleep, snuggled deeply into their mother's warm fur.

The mother beaver snacks on a twig while her kits nurse (drink milk) at her belly.

35

When startled, a white-tailed deer raises its tail like a flag to warn other deer of danger.

A mother deer stands quietly among the tall grasses, surveying the lakeshore.

The beaver family's lodge is like an island in the middle of the lake. Surrounded by deep water, the lodge is out of the reach of foxes, wolves, and other large predators.

Other lake dwellers are not so safe. They must constantly be on guard for danger. Back on shore, a white-tailed deer appears among the trees. The deer's nose twitches as she sniffs the air. Slowly, the deer walks toward the lake. Every few feet she stops to sniff, look, and listen for signs of a predator.

At the water's edge, the deer cautiously looks around. Finally she makes a soft coughing sound. See where the grasses are moving? A tiny spotted fawn steps out into the open. It comes down to join its mother at the water's edge. The mother deer stands guard as her fawn bends down for a long, cool drink.

A white-spotted fawn steps into the cool water for a drink.

The lake is a source of water and food for deer and many other land animals. The largest visitors are moose. On the other side of the lake, a moose has come to drink and to munch on tender water plants.

The moose is a big, bold eater. It walks right out into the lake to reach plants growing in the shallows. It sticks its head underwater and comes up with a mouthful of green. The moose chews slowly, while water streams down its hairy chin.

A hungry moose wades into the lake (top right) *and plunges its head into the water* (middle right). *The moose comes up with a mouthful of plants and munches away* (bottom right and far right).

Moose have big feet
with split hooves that
give them a good grip
as they walk across
muddy lake bottoms.

A bright-eyed water vole takes a big bite out of a juicy plant stem.

The moose leaves big tracks in the mud at the edge of the lake. There are other tracks here too. They are the footprints of smaller animals that have come to the lake to eat and drink.

The tiniest tracks were made by water voles and shrews. Plump, furry water voles move quickly and quietly around the lake all day, slipping unseen through the gently swaying grasses. They eat leaves, roots, and seeds.

A shrew darts down to the water's edge for a quick drink. Then it zips back into the grasses to continue hunting for food. The shrew eats bugs and spiders and rounds out its menu with worms and slugs. Like all shrews, this one eats more than its own weight in food every day!

A hungry water shrew has no trouble eating a worm that's longer than it is.

Air bubbles cling to a shrew's fur and feet as it dives in search of food.

The padded feet of a fox leave tracks along the lake's muddy shore.

Partly hidden among the tall grasses, a red fox stalks its next meal.

As they scurry around the lake, shrews and voles are hard to spot. Their fur is a mixture of brown, gray, and tan—perfect colors for blending in with tree trunks and dead grasses. Being able to hide well helps shrews and voles stay safe from predators such as foxes.

But a fox has keen senses of hearing and smell. One of these skilled hunters is moving silently through the tall grasses on soft, padded feet. Ever so slowly, it sneaks up on the shrew. Then it suddenly leaps out and pounces! With the shrew in its mouth, the fox trots off into the trees.

42

Overhead, another hunter is looking for dinner. An osprey soars high above the lake. Its sharp eyes scan the water for shadows and ripples—any sign of a fish just beneath the surface.

The osprey spots movement near the beaver lodge. The mother beaver is taking her babies out for an evening swim.

The osprey also spies a large trout not far from the beaver family. The bird hovers for a moment. Then it folds its broad wings and dives, with daggerlike talons outstretched.

An osprey's sharp, curved talons are ideal tools for catching fish.

An osprey swoops down toward the water with its talons spread wide.

The loud slap of the beaver's tail warns that danger is near.

The mother beaver sees the osprey dropping like a stone from the sky. Alarmed, she brings her broad, flat tail down hard on the water. *SLAP!* The kits dive instinctively. Their mother is right behind them. In the blink of an eye, the beaver family vanishes beneath the water's surface.

Beating broad wings, the osprey rises from the lake with a fish (top). The beavers bob safely to the surface with wet fur that glistens in the sun (below).

The trout is not quite fast enough. Too late, it sees the shadow of the diving osprey. The osprey rises from the water with a loud cry, holding tightly to its catch. It flies off to its nest high in a nearby tree, where its hungry chicks are waiting for their dinner.

One by one, the beaver kits bob to the surface. The danger has passed. They are safe once again. Until the sun fades from the sky, they will swim and play in the sparkling waters of their lake.

for further
Information
about Lakes

Books

DuTemple, Lesley A. *North American Moose.* Minneapolis, MN: Lerner Publications Company, 2001.

Grimm, Phyllis W. *Crayfish.* Minneapolis, MN: Lerner Publications Company, 2001.

Kalbacken, Joan. *White-tailed Deer.* Chicago: Children's Press, 1992.

McEvey, Shane F. *Dragonflies.* Philadelphia, PA: Chelsea House, 2001.

Patent, Dorothy Hinshaw. *Ospreys.* New York: Clarion Books, 1993.

Pratt-Serafini, Kristin Joy. *Salamander Rain: A Lake and Pond Journal.* Nevada City, CA: Dawn Publications, 2000.

Reid, George K. *Pond Life: A Guide to Common Plants and Animals of North American Ponds and Lakes.* New York: St. Martin's Press, 2001.

Ross, Michael Elsohn. *Pond Watching with Ann Morgan.* Minneapolis, MN: Carolrhoda Books, Inc., 2000.

Schuler, Judy. *Foxes for Kids.* Minocqua, WI: NorthWord Press, 1997.

Silverstein, Alvin, Virginia Silverstein, and Laura Silverstein Nunn. *Photosynthesis.* Brookfield, CT: Twenty-First Century Books, 1998.

Stewart, Melissa. *Life in a Lake.* Minneapolis, MN: Lerner Publications Company, 2003.

Turner, Matt. *Beavers.* Chicago, IL: Raintree Steck-Vaughn, 2004.

Winner, Cherie. *Trout.* Minneapolis, MN: Carolrhoda Books, Inc., 1998.

Websites

Enchanted Learning—Pond
< http://www.allaboutnature.com/biomes/pond/pondlife.shtml >

This website on biomes has lots of information about the animal life found in ponds and lakes.

What's It Like Where You Live?—Ponds and Lakes
< http://mbgnet.mobot.org/fresh/lakes >

Check out this site for information on lake biomes, from how they can form to what plants and animals live in them.

Photo Acknowledgments

The images in this book are used with the permission of: © Bill Banaszewski/Visuals Unlimited, pp. 4–5; © Tom and Pat Leeson, pp. 5, 12 (top), 13; © Gerald and Buff Corsi/ Visuals Unlimited, pp. 6, 12 (bottom); © John Gerlach/ Visuals Unlimited, pp. 7, 17; © D.S. Kerr/Visuals Unlimited, p. 8 (bottom left); © James P. Rowan, pp. 8 (top right), 10 (bottom), 15; © Karlene V. Schwartz, p. 8 (bottom right); © Gary Meszaros/Photo Researchers, pp. 9, 18; © David Wrobel/ Visuals Unlimited, p. 10 (top); © Adam Jones/Visuals Unlimited, p. 11; © David Sieren/Visuals Unlimited, p. 14; © Michael P. Gadomski/Photo Researchers, p. 16; © Gary Meszaros/Visuals Unlimited, p. 19 (left); © G.L. Twiest/Visuals Unlimited, p. 19 (top right); © Glenn M. Oliver/Visuals Unlimited, p. 19 (bottom right); © Wally Eberhart/ Visuals Unlimited, p. 20; © Roger Treadwell/ Visuals Unlimited, p. 21; © John D. Cunningham/Visuals Unlimited, p. 22 (top); © Gary W. Carter/Visuals Unlimited, p. 22 (bottom); © L. West/Photo Researchers, p. 23; © Alan and Sandy Carey/Photodisc by Getty Images, Inc., p. 24; © Tom J. Ulrich/Visuals Unlimited, p. 25; © Anthony Mercieca/Photo Researchers, p. 26; © Jack Fields/Photo Researchers, p. 27; © State of Minnesota, Department of Natural Resources, p. 28 (top); © Maslowski/Photo Researchers, p. 28 (bottom); © Tom McHugh/Steinhart Aquarium/Photo Researchers, p. 29; © John Mitchell/Photo Researchers, p. 30; © Leonard Lee Rue III/Visuals Unlimited, p. 31; © Royalty-Free/CORBIS, p. 32; © Bill Beatty, p. 33; © Ned Therrien/Visuals Unlimited, p. 34; © Tom and Pat Leeson/Photo Researchers, p. 35; © William J. Weber/Visuals Unlimited, p. 36; © Rob and Ann Simpson/Visuals Unlimited, p. 37; © Patrick J. Endres, p. 38 (top); © Francis/Donna Cardwell/Visuals Unlimited, p. 38 (middle); © James L. Davis/Visuals Unlimited, pp. 38 (bottom), 39; © Niall Benvie/CORBIS, p. 40; © Donald Rubbelke, p. 41; © Ron Spomer/Visuals Unlimited, p. 42; © Fritz Pölking/Visuals Unlimited, pp. 43, 45 (top); © Len Rue, Jr., p. 44; © Leonard Lee Rue III, p. 45 (bottom).

Front cover photos by © Len Rue, Jr. (beaver/foreground) and © Karlene V. Schwartz (lake/background).

Index Numbers in **bold** refer to photos and drawings.